AGING WITH GRACE — Strength & Self-Love

— A Life Guide —

AGING WITH GRACE — Strength & Self-Love

— A Life Guide —

Dr. Suzanne Gelb, Ph., JD

FIRST EDITION

All rights reserved. This book or any portion thereof may not be reproduced or used in any manner whatsoever without the express written permission of the publisher except for the use of brief quotations in a book review.

Copyright © 2019 Dr. Suzanne J. Gelb, Ph.D., J.D.

Manufactured in the United States of America.

ISBN-13: 978-1-950764-06-8
ISBN-10: 1-950764-06-0

www.DrSuzanneGelb.com

PRAISE FOR... THE LIFE GUIDES

The author wrote this life guide on aging with grace, strength and self-love, as well as 10 other life guides on various topics, to help readers successfully navigate some of life's trickiest challenges.

Each Life Guide includes educational information sourced from the author's three-plus decades of coaching and counseling in the field of emotional wellness.

What Readers Are Saying

At age 46 (8 years ago), my husband of 20 years, left me for a 22 year old – claiming I was too old for his tastes. I've worked hard to push past all those self-loathing emotions but your Guide really helped at a much deeper level. I'm feeling the love!

I have forgiven him but I realized I haven't forgiven myself. Hence I just purchased your Forgiveness Guide.

I'm eager to delve in! Thank you for your great work."

—Beth

"I never thought I'd say it, but after reading this guide I can say, "I love my aging skin' and "I am not damaged goods." No more disgust and shame. Now I'm convinced that I don't need to be a photoshopped, skinny, flawless woman to be desirable. I am Me — wise, beautiful, sexy. At any age, shape or size.

—Shelly S

"Learning how to love yourself and treat yourself kindly — even when your life, career, body, and relationships aren't 'totally perfect' — is one of the hardest things to do.

Dr. Suzanne Gelb breaks down the art of self-love into practical steps. No woo-woo vagueness. Just easy-to-follow exercises pulled from her 28-year career in the field.
If you're looking for practicality and effectiveness, these Life Guides are a steal of a deal."

—Susan Hyatt, Master Certified Life Coach, Published Author

"Your guidebooks are gems."

—Alexandra Franzen, Published Author, Writing Teacher

CONTENTS

Disclaimer   xiii

INTRODUCTION

Change How You Feel About Aging, Change How You Feel About Your Life.   1

WHAT'S INSIDE AND HOW TO USE THIS GUIDE   6

PART 1

Negative Attitudes About Aging: Is There Really a "Fix?"   7

PART 2

How To Release Negative Emotional Energy — Safely and Effectively.   18

PART 3

Self-Loathing or Healthy Self-Pride? How To Tell the Difference — and Stop Self-Loathing in its Tracks.   29

PART 4

What Does Your True Self Want To Tell You? How To Write a Love Letter to Your Body.   42

PART 5

"You Matter. Deeply." How To Restore Your Self-Worth.   49

PART 6

"Who Do You Want To Be?" Writing a Story About the Kind of Older Person You Want To Become.   55

PART 7

The SHINE List! Older Folks Who Shine Brightly — and Inspire Me, Deeply.   61

A FEW FINAL WORDS

Love Is What You Deserve. Love Is Where You Belong.   65

MORE TIPS, MORE TOOLS

8 FAQs About Inner Battles With Aging.   69

WHAT'S NEXT

Resources… to Keep Learning and Growing.   101

ABOUT THE AUTHOR   108

OTHER BOOKS BY THE AUTHOR   109

INDEX   111

DISCLAIMER

This book is a tool that can help you to shift the way that you feel about aging... so that you can enjoy your life now and in the future.

This book contains educational exercises and tips drawn from my career in the field of emotional wellness with over 30 years of experience. This book is for informational purposes only, and is not intended to diagnose or treat any illness, nor is it a substitute for professional or psychological advice, diagnosis, or treatment. Always consult a qualified health care professional before engaging in any new, self-help resource (such as this one) and with questions you may have about your health and wellbeing.

Any case material that may be alluded to in this book, including in articles, or in interviews [see Resources section] does not constitute guarantees of similar outcomes for the reader. No results can be promised, since everyone's personal development path is unique. Names and details have been changed for privacy.

Links inside this book to external websites are for informational purposes only. Linking does not imply endorsement of or affiliation with that site, its content, or any product or service it may offer.

All link URLs in this book are current at the time of printing. Link URLs may fail at some point if the page has been deleted or moved. The author assumes no responsibility or liability for broken links.

This concludes the disclaimer portion of this book.

Thank you. Enjoy this Guide ... and enjoy your life.

INTRODUCTION

Change How You Feel About Aging, Change How You Feel About Your Life.

Welcome to The Life Guide on AGING WITH GRACE, Strength and Self-Love.

If you picked up a copy of this Guide, chances are you might be feeling a swirl of emotions right now.

You might be feeling …

— Afraid.

(How can I be… so OLD?! I'm not ready for this stage of my life, and I'm scared. Time is passing too quickly.)

— **Angry.**

(I feel like I'm at war with my body. Things are wrinkling, puckering, sagging... it's unfair.)

— **Disgusted.**

(I'm not happy when I look in the mirror, or when I see my reflection in a store window. I can't believe that's me. I don't feel as "aged" as I look.)

— **Betrayed.**

(I take good care of my body, but it is STILL letting me down. I feel creaky, cranky, hormonal, or just plain old exhausted... I want the younger body I used to have.)

— **Invisible.**

(Nobody even glances at me when I walk down the street. It's a young person's world, and I feel like I don't even exist anymore.)

— **Frustrated.**

(I just don't feel good in my clothes, and I don't like being seen in photos...)

If you're having feelings like these, I can relate.

As a psychologist and life coach with a combined total of 3+ decades in the field of emotional wellness, you'd think that I would be "immune" to moments of...

Self-Criticism.

But... I haven't always been.

I remember not that long ago...

Looking in the mirror and thinking...

Is that MY body?! Where did those wrinkles come from? What on earth is happening?!

In that moment, I was filled with so **many negative attitudes and feelings**.

It took me several days to bring myself back into a state of **acceptance and self-love,** but thanks to the emotional "toolkit" that I've built over the years, I was able to do it.

Through that experience, I realized:

I am not alone, with how I'm feeling. Millions of older people, as well as people who are heading into their later years, struggle to remain confident and self-loving in the face of aging.

Happily, I was able to resolve my **negative emotions** and **attitudes** about my **aging** body **relatively quickly**, but...

Other people, who lack decades of experience doing this kind of work, might struggle a great deal more.

This breaks my heart. I want to help.

That experience was the catalyst for writing this Life Guide on aging — a topic very near and dear to my heart.

I hope that this Life Guide provides you with three gifts:

1. **Practical tools** that...

   You can use to **release negative attitudes and feelings about aging** — instead of turning all of that negativity against yourself with debasing self-talk that **degrades your self-image and quality of life**.

2. **A big reminder** that...

   How you feel about your life, and **how you live your life, is in your hands.**

   You don't have to adhere to anybody else's beliefs about what "aging" means.

   You get to choose for yourself.

3. **Another big reminder** that...

   You are **valuable, important and worthy of Love**, in any body, at any age.

Because Love has no age limit, restrictions or expiration date.

We've got lots to cover, and, besides, we're not getting any younger. :)

Let's begin!

What's Inside and How To Use This Guide

Inside this Life Guide, you'll find a series of lessons to support you in shifting the way that you feel about aging... so that you can **savor your life and body**

— **Today,**

— **Tomorrow,**

and

— **In the years to come.**

The Contents page of this life guide gave you a peek at what's ahead.

PART I

Negative Attitudes About Aging. Is There Really a "Fix?".

We live in a world that idolizes the "young" and "beautiful."

Magazines and TV shows are filled to the gills with images of **young, taut teenagers** and **lithe women in their twenties.**

When an older woman is featured in the media, it's usually paired with language that celebrates how "young" she looks, as if it's the ultimate achievement

(How does this 50-year-old woman stay wrinkle-free?! Read on for her secrets...)

Wouldn't it be great if we started to see significant changes in how older people are portrayed? Think about that for a moment, and....

Ask yourself:

How would I like to see older people portrayed?

What's really important?

What truly matters?

All of that being said…

When it comes to issues of

- Self-worth

- Self-esteem

And

- How you feel about your body

What you hear, see, or read about doesn't have the final say.

You do.

The way that you feel, and the way that you live your life, is up to you.

Your emotional wellbeing is *your* responsibility.

So, if you're:

- **Feeling unhappy about your body and aging**

And

- Your **confidence has plummeted**

You can change that.

You must change that.

The responsibility is yours.

Actually, I think this is wonderful.

It puts the **power back in your hands**.

That's **exciting**... and **empowering**!

One point of clarification:

"Taking responsibility" for your emotions doesn't mean that your goal is to become an emotionless person who never gets upset.

Taking responsibility for your emotions means that if you feel emotions tugging at you, making you feel ill at ease — like...

- **Anger** that gnaws at you

- **Self-criticism** that won't quit

Or

- **Persistent fear**

You then **make an active choice** to:

- **Resolve** those negative emotions

- **Release** them

- **Understand** why they occurred in the first place

And

- **Replace** that **negativity with self-love.**

In the next section, we'll talk more about **how to release negative emotional energy — safely** and **effectively**.

For now, it's time for some **self-reflection to:**

Uncover where some of your negative feelings about aging may have originated from — the core experiences that shaped your current beliefs and attitudes.

This kind of reflection can be incredibly helpful as you begin to **teach yourself to age with grace and self-love.**

Write and reflect.

Fill-in-the-blanks below with some free-association writing to answer **the following questions**:

1. Who (or what) taught me how I am "supposed" to feel about aging?

For example:

My mother, who was terrified with aging and obsessed with maintaining a youthful appearance, at any cost...

Or:

Hmm, I don't know. There was just a time, when I was 30-something, and I looked in the mirror and thought, 'Ew, wrinkles around my eyes! Things spiraled downward from there.

_____

_____

_____

_____

_____

_____

_____

2. Do I really believe what I have been taught about aging... or am I following somebody else's script / ideas / beliefs / attitudes / message?

For example:

No, I do not. I believe that aging is a privilege, not a crisis. That is what my wise, inner self knows to be true.

_____

_____

_____

_____

_____

_____

_____

_____

3. What are some of my biggest fears about aging?

For example:

Not being desirable to my husband.

Being overlooked for opportunities at work.

The fact that I've crossed the halfway point in my life. Thinking about my mortality scares me.

_____

_____

_____

_____

_____

_____

4. The next time I am feeling fearful about my aging body and appearance, what are the most loving WORDS I could possibly say to myself?

For example:

You are beautiful and your life is a miracle.

You have so much to offer the world.

There is no need to be afraid. You are loved.

_____

_____

_____

_____

_____

_____

_____

_____

5. The next time I am feeling fearful about my aging body and appearance, what is the most loving ACTION I could possibly take, to soothe and comfort myself?

For example:

I look in the mirror and look deep into my eyes. I see the depths of my soul in my eyes.

I see my inner beauty... my essence... my agelessness.

I love what I see, in that moment.

I love all of me, in that moment... and always.

_____

_____

_____

_____

_____

_____

_____

_____

Once you have answered these questions — especially the last two questions in the set — you may be feeling:

- Happier

- Lighter

Or

- Calmer

If that's what you're experiencing, that's wonderful.

However... this is only a temporary balm.

In order **to resolve negative attitudes about aging** — attitudes that you may have carried with you, for decades — **it takes more than positive words and a kind action or two.**

It requires **a release of the negative emotions** that are fueling those attitudes (like **self-criticality** and **judgement**, fueled by **self-directed anger**).

And since **emotions are energy**, this release must be expressed safely, in both a verbal and a physical way.

But don't worry:

You won't need boxing gloves or gym equipment to get this kind of physical release!

In the next section of this Life Guide, I'll share with you a process that you can use to **release negative attitudes about aging** — and experience **deep calm and peace**.

All you'll need is:

— A hand towel

— A pillow

And

— A private space (it could be your study, even the bathroom if need be, or your garage.) where you have privacy and feel safe.

We'll continue with this, and more, in Part Two.

PART 2

How To Release Negative Emotional Energy — Safely and Effectively. [A Three-Step Process.]

Have you seen what very little kids do when they are hungry, tired, afraid or uncomfortable?

Little kids express their feelings physically.

They may cry, kick, or pound on a soft surface (like a crib) until they've completely released all of the emotional energy that needs to be released.

This is a very natural process for moving emotions through and out of your body.

And it's a process that you can mirror — albeit, in a more "grown-up" way — when you need to **release emotional energy**, too.

Right now, I'm going to share a three-step process that has helped lots of people, and it can help you as well, to release emotions in a healthy way — rather than have those emotions get "stuck" or "bottled up" inside of you, where they may…

- Fester

and

- Cause you to feel pretty badly about yourself

Emotional release: a three-step process.

— **Do you get mad or disgusted, just about every time you look in the mirror?**

Or

— **Do you always find fault with something about your looks? Like:**

Ugh, my hair looks so limp today, it's really thinning.

Or:

More crows feet around my eyes! Gross!

It's **not natural** to live with that type of negativity.

It's not in your genes.

You didn't inherit it...

And **you'd be wise to release it**.

An effective way to achieve this kind of release, in my opinion (and backed by my research) is to **discharge this emotional energy — safely, verbally** and **physically,** and **in private.**

Here's what to do.

Step 1: Catharsis.

Grab a pillow and a hand-towel.

Tie a knot in one end of the towel.

Situate yourself in a private space, where you'll be uninterrupted for a few moments.

It could be your study, even the bathroom if need be, or your garage. Lock the door, if you can.

Then, **focus your thoughts on your body**, for a moment... on your looks... your wrinkles... your aging self.

How do you feel?

I don't want to put words in your mouth, but if you feel anything, it will probably be **anger** and / or **fear**.

Anger

Let's explore first, **what to do with anger**.

To discharge that anger, pound the pillow with the knotted end of the towel.

While you're doing this, **verbalize** how you're feeling.

For example:

If you're angry at your aging body, you might say:

Ugh, you look so old. Gross! Nobody's going to want you!

Or.

Simply repeat:

I don't like you!

I don't like you!

I don't like you!

Keep **pounding** the pillow and **verbalizing** how you feel.

Your words may change, and the focus of your anger might change — perhaps to an earlier time when you didn't feel desirable or wanted.

Don't analyze what you're saying or second-guess yourself.

Trust yourself.

Trust that you're expressing **exactly what you need to**.

Trust that this expression is being guided by your **inner wisdom**.

You're not making this up.

You'll know when to stop. Either because:

— You have a time limit (e.g., you need go and to pick the kids up from school)

Or

— You'll just know — you'll feel that you've gotten to a point where you're complete or you want to pause.

That's a quick overview of how you can release anger, safely.

(Again, in psychological terms, this process is called "**catharsis**.")

Fear

The **same principles** apply for **releasing fear, safely**.

Your fear might sound something like:

My skin is sagging, I'm not sexy or desirable anymore. My spouse is going to want someone younger.

This time, instead of pounding your pillow, **gently hold the pillow up to your face**.

Then **think about whatever you're afraid of**.

Hold that image in your mind, and let yourself scream into the pillow. **Scream all of your fear into the pillow** (fortunately, it will muffle the sound.)

This is an effective way to release this kind of emotional energy. Once you feel complete with releasing your:

- Anger

- Fear

Or

Whatever negative emotions you're feeling…

You can move on to **Step 2** of our 3-step process.

Step 2: Correlation.

The next step in the process is to correlate — to **connect the dots**, so to speak, and **determine what is fueling your feelings**. The root cause.

When you're feeling angry or afraid about:

- **Aging**

Or about:

- **A particular aspect of the aging process**

   (like, not feeling attractive or desirable)

Ask yourself the following question:

When have I felt this way before?

Trust whatever age comes to mind.

It might be one or two years old.

It might be 10 or 15 years old.

Perhaps someone said something to you back then that caused you to feel **ugly** or **unattractive**.

Perhaps someone did something that caused you to think that you **weren't pretty, or handsome**.

Or

Perhaps you were raised by your grandma, whom you adored, and she often complained about how old she was, and that rubbed off on you.

Invariably, if you keep asking yourself this question:

When have I felt this way before?

You'll make some connection with something that occurred during the **first six years of life**.

This makes sense, since that's when **our basic attitudes about ourselves and life are formed**.

We're like a sponge during those **early years**, absorbing everything we see and learn about life... from our caregivers and our surroundings.

You will probably make some kind of connection, or have some memory of something that contributed to how you're feeling now, even though that was a long time ago.

With that in place, you're ready for the **next step in this emotional healing process**:

Rewriting the script (or, in more formal terms, **insight** and **behavior change**.)

One side note, before we move on:

Sometimes, when people ask themselves,

When have I felt this way before?...

Nothing comes to mind at that moment.

If that happens to you, that's **totally OK**.

What many people find, is that **an answer often pops into their mind a bit later.**

Step 3: Rewrite the script.

Hopefully, by now, you have some **insight** into the circumstances that built your **current attitudes and feelings** about the **aging** process.

Ah, my grandma was always complaining about her age. I think and sound just like her when I moan about my age! No wonder!

Armed with these insights, **you're ready to "rewrite the script."**

In other words, you are ready to:

- **Change your thinking**

Which most likely will then prompt

- **Changes your behavior**

Your rewrite might resemble something along these lines:

That was then, this is now. I'm no longer that young child, absorbing everything my grandma said.

That was her script — it's not mine.

I can replace that negative script with a new, healthier message:

That aging is a beautiful privilege, not a handicap.

You can apply this three-step process — **Catharsis, Correlation, Rewriting the Script** — to any negative emotion you may be experiencing.

Any emotion that is

— **Exaggerated**

— **Excessive**

— **Making you uneasy**

Or

— **Uncomfortable**,

Or

— Just plain **won't let up**!

PART 3

Self-Loathing or Healthy Self-Pride? How To Tell the Difference — and Stop Self-Loathing in its Tracks.

You can exercise for thirty minutes because:

— You love your body and want to treat it with respect.

Or

You can exercise for thirty minutes because:

— You detest your body and want to punish yourself.

You can treat yourself to a new concealer or foundation because :

— You enjoy enhancing your body and maximizing your looks.

Or

You can buy a new concealer or foundation because:

— You feel ugly and want to hide, cover yourself up, or become somebody else.

Same actions. Very different motivations.

When it comes to buying products, exercising, getting dressed and "looking your best," are you primarily driven by:

— Self-loathing and fear...

Or By

— Healthy self-pride and self-love?

In this section, I'll share a few insights to help you discover **what's really motivating you**... along with a **guided meditation** to support you in shifting back into **a more loving state of mind.**

Understanding your habits.

Habits are awesome when they're the **good** kind — like:

— Brushing your teeth regularly

— Being punctual

— Eating slowly and mindfully.

It's the "bad" habits we want to watch out for — like:

— Worrying about what others think

— Obsessing about the future

Or

— Getting lost in a sea of self-criticism.

These kinds of habits can take us down, really fast — and keep us down.

Explore the following questions to determine what fuels your everyday habits:

- Fear, criticality, self-loathing?

Or

- Healthy self-pride and self- love?

Write and reflect.

Fill-in-the-blanks with some free-association writing to answer the following questions:

1. First thing in the morning when you look in the mirror, what goes through your mind?

— A fearful, critical thought?

(People won't like how I look. There's another ugly wrinkle!)

Or

— A loving, encouraging thought?

(Hi gorgeous!)

_____

_____

_____

_____

_____

_____

2. When you see yourself naked in the mirror (dare to look!) what do you think?

— A fearful, critical thought?

(Oh my gosh, what are people going to think? Ugh, look at those saggy thighs. No way am I wearing a swim suit!)

Or

— A loving, encouraging thought?

(It's OK that my body is not perfect. I love my body, no matter what!)

_____

_____

_____

_____

_____

_____

_____

3. When you see a person whose considerably younger than you, what goes through your mind?

— A fearful, critical thought?

(No one's going to pay attention to me. I'm really over the hill. I'd give anything to look that young again!)

Or

— A loving, encouraging thought?

(I admire their vibrant, youthful energy and I also love my zest for life and my wisdom — something I didn't have when I was younger.)

_____

_____

_____

_____

_____

_____

_____

4. When you go shopping for clothes or beauty / skincare products, what's your motivation? Fear or Love?

— Fear:

I need to camouflage my sagging, wrinkled skin, it will turn people off.

— Love:

I can't wait to buy something tasteful, comfortable, that I just love.

_____

_____

_____

_____

_____

_____

_____

_____

In answering these questions, you may find that you're driven by fear and self-loathing, a lot... or, a lot more than you'd like!

This means that you still have some negative attitudes and feelings about aging that need to be resolved.

Meditation

This next exercise can help to release some of those **self-limiting beliefs** and **fear-driven thoughts** that you may be experiencing.

It's **a guided meditation**, and you'll need privacy, and about 5 minutes of quiet, uninterrupted time to complete it.

Get yourself a comfortable position, either sitting up or laying down.

Close your eyes.

Let your eyelids gently rest on your eyes.

Take a deep breath in... breathing in oxygen... breathing in life... nurturing every cell in your body.

As you exhale, feel yourself relaxing deeply. Letting go of any negative thoughts... just let them go.

Once again, take a deep breath in... feel the relaxation.

As you exhale, make a sound ["Haaaaaa"] or sigh deeply... letting go of limiting beliefs... **letting go of self-criticality.**

Good. Feel yourself relaxing deeper.

One more time. Inhale deeply...

And then you exhale, make a sound ["Haaaaaa"] or sigh deeply... letting go of limiting beliefs... letting go of self-criticality.

Relaxing deeply.

It is time to:

— Release limiting beliefs about aging.

It's time to:

— Recognize the beauty of all the experiences that you've had over the years

And to:

— Honor your body for enabling you to have had those experiences...

And to:

— Enjoy all the growth and awareness that the years have offered you.

It is time to:

— Honor your body...

And to:

— Love your body exactly how it is.

Because it's:

— Your body.

Because it's:

— Deserving of your love.

Rather than **feeling victimized by aging**…

It is time to:

— **Embrace life.**

Embrace the privilege of life.

— Celebrate your life.

Instead of focusing on what you **don't have** (like a youthful complexion, perhaps)

— Focus on what you do have.

(There's always something to be **grateful** for)

And focus on:

— What you have done with your life.

Whatever it is that's causing you to **fear aging** or to berate yourself for looking "old"…

No longer applies to you.

It is time to:

— Recognize where you picked up these limiting beliefs about aging

(from your **upbringing**, for example, or from **things you've seen, heard, watched and read.**)...

Those beliefs which say:

— You're not attractive enough,

Or

— You're not worthy of being loved.

It is time to:

— Recognize that your limiting beliefs are tied to **someone else's script**

(such as parents, caregivers, things you've seen, heard, watched and read).

It is time to:

— **Release those limiting beliefs**.

It is time to **rewrite the script about aging**...

— A script that **shifts you into your truth** now...

— A script that says,

Even though I may not like my wrinkles, I love my body, unconditionally.

Even though I may not like my saggy skin or overweight tummy, I appreciate my body, unconditionally.

Period.

My body is beautiful.

Period.

A script that shifts you back to a **calm center** within yourself.

A place within yourself where you are **one with yourself**.

Total self-acceptance ...

No.

Matter.

What.

Total peace.

Now take a deep breath in.

And as you exhale, feel yourself **becoming more energized**.

Again, take another deep breath in.

And as you exhale, feel yourself **becoming aware of your body** — your feet, legs, torso, hands, fingers.

Every beautiful inch of you.

One more time, inhale deeply.

Exhale completely.

And when you're ready, you can open your eyes and adjust to the light in your environment, feeling:

— **Calm**

— **Peaceful**

And

— **Energized.**

Welcome back.

PART 4

What Does Your True Self Want To Tell You? How To Write a Love Letter to Your Body.

Your **True Self** is…

Your wisest, calmest, most loving self.

Your **True Self** is…

The version of you that only wants the best for you.

The version of you that only wants to encourage you.

The version of you that is pure Love.

If your **True Self** were sitting right here, right now, guiding you with so much love...

What would that Self say?

Would your True Self say:

— *You are old, ugly and worthless...?*

Or

Would your True Self say:

— *You are important.*

— *You are wise.*

— *You are a miracle.*

— *You have so much to give, so many ways you can serve, just by listening, caring, offering insights or telling a story.*

— *Such value and beauty.*

— *Just by existing.*

— *Just by being...*

— *You?*

Whatever your True Self would say?

Say that to yourself.

Soak it up.

Believe it.

Because whatever your True Self is saying... is the truth.

Right now, it's time to write a love letter to yourself and to your body.

Write the letter from the perspective of your **True Self**, in all of its **brilliance**.

As if your True Self is:

- Your best friend

- A wise teacher

Or

- A loving mother or father

Writing a beautiful letter to you.

You can write whatever you like, but …

If you need a little nudge to get the words flowing, try using this **fill-in-the-blank** script.

Dear [insert name],

Did you know that you are a miracle?

You are a miracle because

_____

_____

_____

_____

Did you know that **you are beautiful**?

When I look at your body, I see **incredible beauty**.

I see your

_____

_____

_____

_____

And your

_____

_____

_____

_____

And your strong, amazing

_____

_____

_____

_____

Did you know that **you matter**?

You matter to so many people.

You matter to

_____

_____

_____

_____

because

_____

_____

_____

_____

You matter to

_____

_____

_____

_____

because

_____

_____

_____

_____

Never doubt for a moment that you are valuable and that the world needs you, just as you are.

Did you know that **you were born to love and be loved?**

Did you know that there is an **endless wellspring of love inside of you** that will never run out?

In this endless well, **there is enough love** to give to other people and to yourself, forever.

Things may occasionally block the waters from flowing, but you can remove those obstacles with the **new tools** you are learning.

You have that power and no one can take it away.

Did you know that you can give love to yourself, unconditionally, just as a mother loves her child?

You can.

The next time you feel frightened, uneasy, angry or upset about growing older, I want you to read this letter to yourself, to **remember your true nature: Love.**

Love,

Your True Self

PART 5

"You Matter. Deeply." How To Restore Your Sense of Self-Worth and Value.

I just feel invisible. Like I don't matter anymore.

This is one of the most heartbreaking things that any person can say.

Sadly, I hear different iterations of this statement frequently. Often, from friends and clients who are middle-aged or in their later years.

A moment ago, in Part 4, you wrote yourself a beautiful Love Letter. Direct from your True Self.

This letter may have **restored your sense of self-worth**. At least, for a little while.

But if negative feelings of "worthlessness" are creeping back in, this most likely means that you have more negative emotions that you need to release, so that Love can do its work.

It doesn't mean that any emotional release that you did in Part Two was ineffective, or didn't last.

It just means that there's another layer of emotions... a deeper layer.

Personal Growth Work and Healing Is Often Like Peeling the Layers of an Onion. One Layer at a Time.

So, when you're ready, consider revisiting **Part 2** of this Life Guide and following the **3-step process** once again:

1. Catharsis

2. Correlation

3. Rewriting the Script

So that you can:

Give Yourself Love and Healing.

So that you can:

Soothe the Child You Once Were, Even More ... Your Inner Child.

Because your inner child is the part of you that:

Feels Invisible and Like You Don't Matter.

The part of you that:

Needs Nurturing.

The part of you that:

Needs To Hear You Say,

"I See You. You Matter to Me."

By **loving and comforting your inner child**, you can allow that part of you to "grow up" — so that it can merge with your adult self.

Then, you can **feel whole and complete**.

Every part of you can **feel grown-up and strong**.

In doing this, you are rewriting the script that you currently follow, **shifting from negativity into love.**

From:

"I'm not... I can't... I won't..."

To

"I Am... I Can... I Will..."

If you don't feel like going through the 3-step process right now — don't feel like pounding a pillow, or verbalizing how you feel — that's OK.

Do it later, whenever you're ready.

In the meantime?

This short story may provide some hope and comfort.

My Story: "Continue To Love Yourself."

Years ago, when I was at one of my lowest points — feeling insignificant and hopeless — I had the privilege of working with some masterful spiritual teachers.

And at the end of every session, no matter what we had just worked on, or how I was feeling, they would always say,

"Continue to love yourself as much as we love you."

And often, during the sessions, they would say,

"Love yourself as much as you want to be loved."

I couldn't always grasp the full meaning of these statements, because I was wallowing in my own negativity — fear, guilt, shame, blame and deep insecurity.

But somewhere, somehow, I "heard" the words.

And they helped me.

"Continue to love yourself..."

I think about these words, almost daily.

These words have been comforting and nurturing to me, and to many clients I've worked with as well.

I hope that these words will be helpful to you, when you're feeling like you don't matter.

Because you do.

You Have a Beautiful Light Within You.

A light that is:

Capable of Shining Brilliantly.

A light that can really:

Make a Difference in the World.

Let's sing to that, as we enjoy an excerpt from a gospel song written for children in the 1920s by Harry Dixon Loes.

The song is called, "This little light of mine."

This little light of mine

I'm going to let it shine

Oh, this little light of mine

I'm going to let it shine

This little light of mine

I'm going to let it shine

Let it shine, all the time, let it shine

Continue To Shine.

Continue To Love.

PART **6**

"Who do you want to be?" Writing a story about the kind of older person you want to become.

When you were a child or a teenager, did you have big dreams about the kind of life you might have... once you were "all grown up"?

"I'm going to live in a beautiful house by the sea..."

"I'm going to teach and write books full of magical stories..."

"I'm going to become a doctor and help people get well..."

"I'm going to have three children of my own..."

"I just want to be happy."

Maybe all of your big, beautiful dreams came true.

Maybe different, equally beautiful dreams came true.

Maybe life didn't go the way that you'd hoped.

No matter what happened, or didn't happen... right now? It's time to:

Dream a New Dream.

It's time to:

Create a New Vision for the Kind of Life You Want To Lead... Now That You're a "Really Grown-Up Grown Up."

Ready?

Fill in the blanks to write a new story about the kind of "older person" that you want to become. Starting today.

My Best Life. My New Story.

In my new story...

I wake up at

_____

_____

and I greet the day by

_____

_____

I live in

_____

_____

and my home feels like

_____

_____

My days are full of

_____

_____

and

_____

_____

I make

_____

_____

a priority, and I lovingly say "no" to things that drain me, like

_____

_____

and

_____

_____

If negative emotions flood me, my first response is to

_____

_____

rather than

_____

_____

I rarely

_____

_____

anymore, because now I know better.

Now I Have the Tools To Take Better Care of Myself.

I contribute to my family / my community / the world by doing

_____

_____

and by being

_____

_____

I know that I matter because

_____

_____

I Treat Myself With Unconditional Love and Respect, and This Love Flows From Me Into Everything I Do and Say.

I fall asleep each night feeling

_____

_____

I don't feel "old," I feel

_____

_____

PART 7

The SHINE List! Older people who shine brightly — and inspire me, deeply.

There are **SO many amazing older people doing amazing things in the world**, but they rarely get celebrated in the way they deserve. I'd like to change that.

Here's a list of a few older people who have inspired me, deeply. Men and women who prove that:

Getting Older Can Be a Fabulous Adventure!

May they **inspire YOU to shine even more brightly**, too.:

A Blogger.

I especially love Olive Riley's story. She's a woman who **started blogging when she was... 107 years old!!**

https://bit.ly/2HdBM10

A Mountain Climber.

And then there's Min Bahadur Sherchan. This man **climbed Mount Everest at age 76**.

His motivation?

To show what the human spirit is capable of — and promote world peace.

https://bit.ly/2VhbG1U

A Sailor.

Can you imagine sailing around the world? The entire world? That's an incredible accomplishment.

Now imagine someone sailing around the world at **age 77** — mind-boggling.

But that's what Minoru Saito did. He is the the **oldest person to sail around the world.**

https://bit.ly/2WCMeFF

A Country Music Artist.

Are you a country music fan?

Even you're not, you're going to want to put your hands together (applaud) this next country music performer.

His name? Smoky Dawson. He is **oldest person to ever release a country music album**!

He released "Homestead of my Dreams" when he was… **92 years old**!!

https://bit.ly/2WCMeFF

From Tennis To Yoga to Singing Opera, These Women Prove That Age Is Just a Number!

Tennis, Track and Field, Pole Vaulting.

Does / did your great grandma hold any world records? Sounds like an odd question, doesn't it?

Not for Flo Meiler. This former senior Olympics tennis player, cut her teeth on track and field at age 60, and was a first time pole-vaulter at age 65.

Ten years later, she **holds 15 world records.**

And to top off her list of accomplishments — she's a great grandma!

https://bit.ly/2uSFL01

Teaching Yoga

Per the Guinness Book of World Records, Bernice Bates is oldest **yoga** teacher in the world. She is **92 years old**!!

She didn't start learning yoga until age 60.

https://bit.ly/1PipqRk

Opera Star

Imagine having an 80 year career on stage and screen — and still going strong at nearly… 93 years old!!

That's the story of Marta Eggerth, a soprano who has appeared in numerous operetta roles, and made some 40 movies.

https://amzn.to/2HeHv82

Aging Gracefully

My list of older people who radiate their beauty, and inspiration would be incomplete without doing an internet search using these, or similar, words:

"Aging gracefully images"

If you do this, here's what you're likely to come across:

Stunning images of **older men**, **women** and **couples**, looking **strong, poised** and **beautiful — inside and out.**

A FEW FINAL WORDS

Love is what you deserve.
Love is where you belong.

As an **unborn child**…

— You Deserved Love.

As an **infant**…

— You Deserved Love.

— As a **toddler**, a **teenager**, a young man or woman in your **twenties** or **thirties**...

— You Deserved Love.

Today, **right now**, in this moment…

— You Still Deserve Love.

You deserve **love from others**, of course.

Along with **attention**, **care** and **respect**.

And — though it doesn't always happen — it's wonderful when you receive it.

But more importantly…

— You Deserve the Kind of Unconditional Love That You Can — and Must — Give to Yourself. The Love That Comes From Within and Never Runs Out.

This is the kind of love that…

— Brings Deep Satisfaction

This is the kind of love that…

— Energizes You

And

— Allows You To Serve Others, Too

And…

This is the kind of love that…

— Allows You To Look at Yourself in the Mirror and Smile, Thinking,

"I Love… Me."

Whether your face is **smooth** or **creased** with age.

Whether your body is **20** years old or **102**.

Whether you feel that you've **accomplished a lot** in your life, or **not enough**.

I hope this Life Guide has helped you to…

Shift Your Perception About What "Aging" Means.

I also hope it has offered you some new tools to…

Manage Negative Emotions

like:

Excessive Anger and Fear

when / if these emotions arise.

I'll leave you with a few words from a very wise woman:

"If you realized how beautiful you are,

you would fall at your own feet."

— Byron Katie [born in 1942. age 71.]

Byron is right.

You Are Beautiful.

You Are a Miracle.

You Matter.

And You Are Not Invisible.

Love, always.

MORE TIPS, MORE TOOLS

FAQs About Inner Battles with Aging.

Being alive, at any age, is truly a privilege. Here are even more tips and tools to continue your journey to replace negative feelings about aging with positive ones

Read on for my answers[1] to some of the more typical questions I've been asked over the past 3+ decades, as I've helped people who were uncomfortable with aging, to **refocus** on what brings them **joy** and look forward a **pleasurable future**.

Here's to life!

---

[1] The questions and answers are summarized here, to maximize your learning experience.

Question No. 1 — Aging Parents

Understanding Why This Can Be Unsettling

My parents are in their 80's with noticeable health problems.

There's talk of putting my dad in a care home, with mom soon to follow.

We don't even know if one or both of them will last long enough to take that next step.

Watching them deteriorate is so sad for me... even though they are in good spirits (all things considered, and also taking into account that dad has a very controlling personality and mom passively tries to cater to everything he wants, or at the very least, she agrees with everything he says.)

My husband and I have two grown children, and three grandkids. But there's something about the "end of life" care "talk" for my parents that is hitting me kind of hard.

I feel so unsettled, and nothing seems to make it go away. I try to distract myself with work and other things and this helps to take my mind off my parents' health, but sooner or later, I'm thinking about my parents again, and this unsettled, uneasy feeling comes right back.

I'm usually pretty in control of how I feel, but I can't shake this unsettled feeling.

What could be making me feel this way?

Response:

There could be many reasons why an adult child might feel unsettled at the thought of their parent / s passing on.

Generally speaking, and what I've often seen in my work with clients around this issue, is that **emotionally**, they feel at a **loss**.

This can feel akin to feeling what I often identify as, "an emotional orphan."

As one client who was dealing with a father was really ill, put it,

"I feel like I'm 3 years old, and I don't have a dad."

In essence, what he uncovered in his work with me on this issue was that he had never truly developed emotional independence.

Meaning: His dad was quite overprotective during his childhood, and even though he matured into a successful adult, personally and professionally, he had never quite resolved that subconscious, **emotional dependency** on her father.

This dependency did not interfere with his ability to develop and mature responsibly. However, the pending loss of his father, or at least the thought of his father's mortality as end-of-life issues arose, caused the client's repressed emotional dependency on his father to surface — and it surfaced in the form of feeling "unsettled" (just like you described) and like an afraid, parentless child.

Soothing the Fear

Once this client had gained some **insight and understanding** as to why he was feeling so vulnerable, I showed him an exercise that he could do to nurture his "inner child" — that part of him that was expressing itself through his frightened emotions.

By doing this exercise, he was able to reassure that scared part of himself (inner child), that he (client) is the father now — which means that the inner child is not alone or parentless.

Peace and Relief

After doing this exercise, the client no longer felt unsettled. In fact, he was surprised at how **at peace** and **relieved** he felt, even though nothing had changed in terms of his father's condition.

Life Is Now a Challenge, Not a Threat

In a follow-up session, he also told me that he was feeling much stronger… and that dealing with his father's illness now felt like a **challenge, and no longer a threat**.

Natural Development

That's essentially how natural development occurs. What I mean is that children are initially dependent on their parents for parenting.

Then, as children develop, if they are raised with **healthy, positive parenting**, they acquire more independence, and they increasingly learn from their parents / role-models how to take care of themselves… until they are **mature enough** (physically, mentally, emotionally, spiritually) to go out into the world, and make it on their own.

If that's the case, then, at a later time, the thought of a parent's mortality **would not be unsettling**.

There may be a few moments of grief, and possibly fear, which is natural when faced with a parent's geriatric issues — but these feelings would **not be excessive**. Instead, they would be **in proportion to the situation**.

This means that any fear that may be experienced, would not rise to the level of "feeling unsettled."

Follow-Up Question: How To Parent the Child I Used To Be

I relate to your example with your client. Sounds like my story.

It feels kind of funny and, childish maybe, to think of talking to a child who I can't see and actually doesn't exist, but I can see how who I was as a child and how I grew up, can still be affecting me as an adult.

Would that exercise about reassuring the child that I was once was, be helpful for me to try, so I can shake this unsettled feeling about my parent's health problems?

Response:

I appreciate your openness. You're absolutely welcome to give that exercise a try, if you'd like. In general, here's how it goes.

An Exercise To Nurture the Inner Child

For this exercise, you'll need:

— A private space — preferably a room in your home.

— At least 5 to 10 minutes.

— No interruptions or disturbances.

— A soft pillow.

Now you're ready to begin...

Sit in a comfortable position with the pillow on your lap.

Close your eyes, letting your eyelids gently rest on your eyes.

Take a deep breath in, as you count in your mind: "1, 2."

Exhale, as you count in your mind: "1, 2."

Repeat.

Take a deep breath in, as you count in your mind: "1, 2."

Exhale, as you count in your mind: "1, 2."

Now, still with your eyes closed, wrap your arms around the pillow, and give it a hug.

As you do this, imagine that it is the child that you once were, who you are hugging.

Allow yourself to feel loving towards this child.

Allow yourself to feel deeply caring for this child.

Then say out loud:

I love you. I'm here to protect you. You are not alone.

I am your parent now. I will never abandon you. You are safe.

You are very special to me. You are loved.

Feel free to repeat these sentences for a second time or as many times as you want to. Or if saying these sentences once only feels sufficient, that's fine too.

This is how you can soothe the emotional part of you that is still a small, scared [unsettled] child.

After that, the child within you can feel **safe** and **trusting of your love and protection**. Then the unsettled [fear] feeling, is likely to dissipate.

Question No. 2 — Loss of Older Generation

I'm in my late 50's. Mom passed last year, and my Dad passed a few weeks ago. My best friend, who's a bit older than me, lost her mother this year, and her dad is quite ill.

So I've been around a lot of loss with the older generation, and it feels like it's staring me in the face that,

"I'm next in line."

It seems like this all crept up on me so fast.... next, my children will be discussing end of life care for me and my husband!"

The thought of that happening is very unsettling to me (hopefully, it won't happen and when it's "my time," I'll pass on peacefully and easily in my recliner, watching my favorite soap opera.)

But just thinking about "if" it were to happen, makes me feel anxious...

I thought I was OK about death and dying, but I must say, thinking that "I'm next" is an adjustment I can't wrap my mind around...

It's like in my mind, my parents were always "there" somehow... and even after Mom passed, Dad was still around. But now he's gone, and others from that preceding generation have gone too.

Yet...

I feel healthy and like I have a lot of living to do, and, I just can't relate to me being "next!" How did this new reality creep up so fast?

How can I make peace with this?

Response:

I can appreciate the **emotional and intellectual adjustment** that's in front of you, as you transition from having lived your entire life with the awareness that **one or both parents were a part of your life** — yet now, they're no longer here.

Which means that **you're now at the helm**, so to speak.

That said…

Although it's important to **responsibly prepare**, as best we can, **for our future** (and that includes making provisions for long-term care, if that's what we choose to do, and making sure that our affairs are in order — health care directives, etc. — it's equally important to **seize the moment**, and **live life fully**.

This means resisting quite a common tendency… which is to dwell on how old we are (age is, after all, just a number) or that "we're next!"

Yes, as mentioned above, we want to responsibly prepare for the future, as we see fit, and take the best care of ourselves in the present as we absolutely can… but beyond that? Well, part of a song comes to mind. It's from the 1956 Alfred Hitchcock film, "The Man Who Knew Too Much."

It goes like this:

"Que será, será

Whatever will be, will be

The future's not ours to see

Que será, será

What will be, will be."

Why did this song come to mind?

Because of these 3 lines:

    1. Whatever will be, will be

    2. The future's not ours to see

    3. What will be, will be

Keeping those 3 lines in mind, can free us up to:

- **Live in the moment,**

- **Not be unnecessarily preoccupied with the future,**

And

- **Enjoy life fully, with no self-imposed limitations because of our age.**

That said, for some people, there may be deeper feelings and issues below the surface, so to speak, that need to be addressed and resolved, because they can fully and completely live the words of that song.

In those instances, professional assistance from a competent, health-care provider could be feasible. Sometimes, when we're feeling strong emotions (e.g., fear), no matter how conscientious we may be about trying to be objective and sort things out, it's hard to "see the forest for the trees." That's where a trained professional may be able to help.

If that feels like a direction you want to pursue, it's best to act on it, sooner rather than later… so that peace can be on the way.

Alternatively, as you stated in your question, you "feel healthy" and you "have a lot of living to do."

This Writing Exercise Can Help.

Fill-in the-blanks to answer the next two questions:

I am healthy. What is stopping me from enjoying my life?

_____

_____

_____

_____

I have a lot of living to do. What is stopping me from living fully?

_____

_____

_____

_____

Now that you have some **insight** and **understanding** into how you may be holding yourself back from fully enjoying your life, it's time to:

- **Shift gears**

And

- **Embrace life for all it has to offer**

This Second Writing Exercise Can Also Help.

Fill-in the-blanks to the next two questions:

I am healthy. From now on, I will enjoy my life by doing

_____

_____

_____

_____

I have a lot of living to do. From now on I'll live life fully by doing

_____

_____

_____

_____

Question No. 3 — Fear of Being a Burden

Accepting Care From Loved Ones

I'm in my 40s but when I think about aging, I have one looming fear — I don't want to be a burden to my family if I get sick and need care when I get older.

I come from a traditional family where we take care of each other. That means even when one of us gets sick.

We don't put family members in care homes unless we really have to. But if we can care for each other at home, that's what we do. It's just the way we are.

I love our family values, but I need help with getting over the worry and fear of being a burden.

How can I get over feeling this way?

Response:

You're not alone in feeling like it's easier to give than to receive (i.e., be given to / cared for). So many people feel this way.

In my experience, that's largely due to **how we were raised**:

- We were taught that it's **better (more noble) to give than to receive**.

- Alternatively that **may not necessarily be the message** that was directly conveyed, but that was our "take-away" based on how we **interpreted** what we observed during childhood.

OK With Giving, But Not With Receiving

Either way, as a result, as adults (and probably also prior to adulthood) we **don't feel too comfortable** with **receiving** (being given to / cared for).

But when it comes to **giving**, especially to family... well that's **second nature** to us.

That said, your question adds another layer to the issue of **discomfort** with **being cared for**. That is, the fear that you'll be a **burden** on the family who is caring for you.

Unfortunately, this is an attitude that is, and has been, somewhat pervasive in society for some time - the fact that ailing elderly people are a burden on society - be that on family caregivers, resources, etc.

Caring for Family Members Can Be Stressful

Some people also pick up this attitude up from within their own families.

It is true that caring for an elderly loved one at home can be very stressful, and sometimes, for example, parents who are caring for their elderly parents in the family home overtly display their **frustration**... in front of their children.

The **elderly family member** is then at risk for feeling like they are a **burden** on the caregiver.

The **children**, being sensitive and perceptive, are **aware of this burdensome feeling**, directly or indirectly.

Consequently, they may be at risk for two factors as they grow up:

1. Emulating their parents and feeling like caring for an ailing family member is a **burden**;

And / or

2. Fearing that if, when they're older, they they need to be cared for by their family, they will be a **burden.**

Have said that, there could be other underlying factors that are causing "fear of being a burden" to be an issue. To identify and resolve those factors, a consultation with a qualified health-care professional may be a feasible next step. If that feels right to you, don't hesitate to reach out to a provider of your choice. Sometimes just one session can make the world of difference.

Wondering what takes place in a therapy session? 189,292 other people have also been wondering.

They have all read my article on this topic, published online in my column, "All Grown Up," on Psychology Today.

The article is called: **"What Actually Happens During A Therapy Session?"**

It includes 6 other common questions about psychotherapy, and can be found here:

https://bit.ly/2HdzRuj

If you don't feel that you need to go as far as seeking counseling, that's great too. Just know that "feeling like a burden" is not something you made up. Nor is it something you were born with. It's an **attitude** or **self-perception** that you have learned a long the way, during your life's journey.

Fortunately, Anything That Has Been Learned Can Be Unleaded and Relearned in a More Self-Supporting, Self-Nurturing Way.

Now that you know **where** or **how** you may have **learned** / or picked up the **self-defeating attitude of feeling like a burden** to your family, it's time to **unlearn that negative message**.

It's time to replace:

— **Low self-esteem** and **lack of self-worth**

With

— **Self-confidence** and **self-respect**.

Try These Affirmations:

I am loving and lovable. I deserve to receive love and loving care.

I deserve to be surrounded by love and caring.

I deserve to be cared for with love.

I deserve to accept help from family members.

When I accept help from family, they're gratified by giving.

When I accept help from family,, they receive my gift of gratitude.

When I accept help from family, I'm affirming their generosity.

Question No. 4 — Fear of Being Uncared For

Sharing Concerns With Family

I'm 66 and in good health. Yes, there are the morning creaks when I get up, and I don't feel good if I "burn-the-candle-at-both-ends" like I used to... but overall, life is good.

I have three adult children. Two of them live nearby and each one has two kids, the third lives in another country.

I love being a grandma, and although my husband and I wish we could see more of our grandkids, we understand how demanding it must be for our children to be working parents. Just raising a family is a full time job!

When it comes to aging, my fear is that, sad to say, no one will want to care for me (aside from my husband, but he's quite a bit older than me, so he might pass first, but that's not for certain).

It's unfortunate, but maybe it's just the way things are, or maybe it's the way I raised my children, but these days, the younger generation seems self-absorbed and "into" themselves. They seem selfish. I'm sorry to say it, but it's what I see... and I'm sorry if I spoiled my kids when they were young, and that's why they're selfish now.

But I'm digressing. My fear — that gets stronger each day as I get older — is that my kids won't want to care of me, if I need care. I'm afraid I'll end up in a facility, alone and not mattering to anyone.

I love my children, but we don't usually have deep talks. How do I talk to them about my fears?

Response:

Opening up the lines of communication with your children is an excellent first step. You may be surprised how much they might **welcome the conversation**, since they were probably unaware of how you were feeling.

But, deep down, we all have love in our hearts, and **we all have the capacity to share that love with others**, to **empathize** when another is hurting or afraid, and to **care**.

Sometimes, the Benefits of Opening Up Communication With Loved Ones Can Be Far Greater Than We Imagined.

Not only do we create the opportunity for **our needs to possibly be met** when we broach the subject and share our concerns with our loved ones, in this instance, but **our loved ones benefit** as well… sometimes in more ways than one.

How?

Example:

Talking to your family, creates an precious opportunity for them to:

— **Share love with you and concern for you**, rather than tending to be "self-absorbed," as you put it.

It always feels good to **share genuine love and concern**. It always feels good when our heart opens.

— **Experience healthy, open communication**. What are gift you are giving to them (and to yourself) by opening up the lines of communication.

It always feels good to **have a heart-to-heart talk with someone**.

It always feels good to really listen and to be understanding.

So, when you're ready…

Take a Few Deep Breaths, To Relax and Calm Yourself.

Then pick up the phone, make that call to your child/ren, and set up a time to talk.

It would be ideal if both your children could be present for this conversation.

And please… have this conversation **in person**, **face-to-face**.

Although technology can be a marvelous communication tool, this **sensitive conversation** — where you share your fears and talk about your later years — is not something that you want to do via text or email.

Trust That:

— Opening up the lines of communication is a beautiful thing.

— You will know what to say.

— All will be well.

Question No. 5 — Becoming a Grandparent

Living Life Fully No Matter What Age We Are

Two months ago we welcomed my first grandchild into the world. She is precious and I'm over the moon with excitement!

But when I visit her, this feeling (dread) sometimes comes over me. It's like, as I look at her, she's so young and has her whole life in front of her, and I'm thrilled for her, but it makes me feel so old... like my life is over... like her life matters and mine doesn't.

Why do I feel this way?

Response:

Sounds like you might be running into some attitudes about aging within yourself that were dormant before the birth of your granddaughter — which is why you weren't aware of feeling the way you do now.

Meaning: It's not uncommon for people to have a conscious or subconscious attitude that youth is **desirable**, and being elderly is **undesirable**. You can probably think of where you might have picked up such an attitude yourself! Media, parents, teachers, etc.

But **you can change that attitude**, now that you are aware of its presence... and aware that it is causing you emotional discomfort.

Why?

Because it is **not natural to have this attitude** — the attitude that youth is preferable to being elderly, and that unless someone is young and vibrant, with many years of living waiting for them, so-to-speak, life is not worth much.

Every Life Matters. Regardless Of Age.

Every Life Is Worth Living. Regardless Of Age.

It is a misnomer that only a young person holds the keys to life. Each breath that a 70-year-old takes is just as significant as each breath that a 7-month-old takes.

So…

Next time you're with your granddaughter and you look into her beautiful eyes, you could **think to yourself:**

— *You're beautiful. And so am I.*

— *You matter. And so do I.*

— *You are a gift to me. And I am a gift to you.*

— *You have much to teach me. And I have much to teach you.*

— *You're worth loving. And so am I.*

— *You have a lot of living to do. And so do I.*

And that's the truth!

Question No. 6 — Feeling Old at Work

Learning To Appreciate Ourselves At Any Age

I've worked at my current job for a lot of years (I won't say the exact number of years, because then I'll give my age away. Let's just say, retirement is not imminent, but I've been giving it some thought!)

When I look around the office these days, there are quite a few young people. I'm good at my job but somehow I feel that these young ones are better, smarter, and that they know more than me because they were in college not that long ago.

And then there's technology...

These young folks have grown up with the internet and all of the techno-gadgets, but I'm not too savvy with all of that (oh dear, I'm kind of revealing my age again.) That's another reason I feel insecure.

I feel outdone by the younger generation. Like what I have to offer isn't much... like maybe I should retire early.

Or sometimes I think that maybe I should go and work somewhere else where there aren't so many young people... maybe then I will feel better about things.

But I like where I work and the job that I do, and I don't want to retire yet.

How can I feel better about all of this?

Response:

First, you may want to challenge yourself admitting to your age, instead of not wanting to reveal it, as you indicate in your question.

As long as we're:

- Ashamed
- Embarrassed
- Self-critical

And / or

- Unaccepting

of whatever age we are, then what is likely to happen is that **it will take very little in our environment** (e.g., younger co-workers) **to trigger our discomfort with our age**.

It Is Time To Reframe How We Think and Feel About Aging.

It is time to:

- Cut ourselves some slack

And to:

- Replace self-judgement with self-acceptance.

This Next Writing Exercise Can Help:

Fill-in the-blanks by finishing the next two statements.

If you need additional space for your writing, grab a sheet of paper and continue on.

Write as much as you want to… the more the better.

Let your thoughts flow…

Let your feelings bubble up to the surface…

Statement Number 1:

I'm ashamed to admit my age because

_____

_____

_____

_____

Example:

I'm **ashamed** to admit my age because I'm not proud of the fact that I look, old, and I'm **embarrassed** that my life has not turned out as I had hoped.

Stress has taken its toll on my appearance, and I have made **mistakes** and **missed opportunities** that I can never go back and reclaim.

Statement Number 2:

It's ok for me to admit my age because

_____

_____

_____

_____

Example:

It's ok for me to admit my age because I am proud of who I am and of the life that I have lived.

Yes, I have made mistakes, but I have learned from those experienced and I am a stronger and wiser person because of this.

I have a lot of living to do. From now on I'll live life fully by doing

_____

_____

_____

_____

This type of exercise has helped many people to be **more accepting** of their **age** and **accomplishments** (or even lack thereof) in their lives.

Sometimes though, **issues about aging can run deep** and it may be wise to consult a healthcare professional for support.

Expecting Ourselves To Keep Up With the "Youngsters"...

Back to your question...

You appear to be putting a lot of pressure on yourself to be "just like" "the young people" in your office, as you put it in your office.

Instead of:

— **Comparing** yourself to them

— **Expecting** yourself to keep up with them

And then

— **Judging** yourself from not being like them

You might consider:

— **Appreciating** the **differences** between yourself and your younger counterparts.

Everyone has value. Everyone has something to share.

Yes, those who have grown up with technology may be more **proficient** with it, but **it's never too late to learn a new skill** (if that's what you choose.)

At the same time, let's not underestimate the value of **knowledge and wisdom** that can only be gained from **experience** — something you appear to have quite a bit of.

So, **instead of competing** with these co-workers, consider **a more complimentary** type of relationship... where you can **learn from them** and they can **learn from you**. Again,

Everyone Has Something To Offer.

Everyone Has Something To Learn.

Wouldn't it be wonderful if, in this type of situation, we:

- Stopped competing to outdo each other

And

- Started sharing our respective resources with each other.

This can happen.

And when it does...

Watch how the **magic, creativity** and **ingenuity** comes forth!

A **true collaboration** of the **best** that everyone has to offer.

Question No. 7 — Retiring

Getting Comfortable With the Idea of Retiring

I've started to plan for retirement.

It will be about another year before I quit my job to retire, but the thought of retiring is a little bit exciting, but mostly unsettling.

I like my routine of going to work, enjoying camaraderie with my colleagues at work, and feeling like I do make a difference, even though I'm not famous… so it's not like I reach millions of people with what I do.

When I think of retiring, one reason it's unsettling is because I have no idea what I want to do when I retire — or if I even want to do anything. I'm embarrassed to say this, but see myself being useless when I retire, rather than useful. It's just a big, blank unknown.

How can I feel good about retiring so that this void (nothingness / uselessness) that I think is waiting for me, when I retire, doesn't spoil what otherwise would be a very exciting time in my life.

Response:

Keep in mind that…

You Are Important And You Matter … No Matter What.

This means that **you are important** and **you matter**, even if you:

— **Do** meaningful work when you retire.

— **Don't do** meaningful work when you retire.

— **Know** what you want to do when you retire.

— **Don't know** what you want to do when you retire.

— **Contribute to** society via your work, when you retire.

— **Don't contribute to** society via your work, when you retire.

You Are Significant, No Matter What.

You Can Receive Love, No Matter What.

You Can Give Love, No Matter What.

Some potential retirees, who kept these affirming statements in mind, found that they were then able to:

— Feel full inside, rather than empty.

— Perceive their future as an adventure, rather than a void.

— Look forward to their future with eager curiosity and optimism.

This type of **mindset** can help you be **excited** about being on the "eve" of your retirement.

Good luck, and enjoy!

Question No. 8 — Turning 65 or Older

Learning to Joyfully Celebrate ALL Birthdays

I just turned 65. I feel so old. In reality, I'm in good health (definitely as healthy as I was when I was 60, let's say), but 65 is so O-L-D..

My friend turned 70 earlier this year. We walk together every day, in the mornings, so I know she's in good health like me. She's usually a positive person with a hopeful outlook on life, but she felt the same way as I do about turning 65.

She told me that this is what went through her mind as her 70th birthday was approaching, and also on her birthday:

"70 sounds so old...., what's to celebrate? Feels like my life is pretty much over."

Is this what I have to look forward to with each upcoming birthday? Am I really too old to have fun and enjoy life?

Response:

Consider this:

— You're as **old** as you think you are.

— You're as **young** as you think you are.

— You may not be able to **stop** the clock, but you can **stop the pessimistic outlook.**

— You may not be able to **turn back the calendar**, but you can **reframe how you think about yourself,** your life, and, yes, your age.

Whether You Accept Your Age, or Label Yourself as "Too Old To Enjoy Life" Is Up to You.

Whether You Accept Your Age, and Don't Allow a Number To Stop You From Enjoying Life, Is Up to You.

Look how much **power** you have, if you choose to **exercise it.**

Look how much **enjoyment awaits you,** if you choose to **enjoy life.**

How We Feel About Ourselves and our Lives, Is a Choice.

— We choose whether we're optimistic, or pessimistic.

— We choose whether we're hopeful, or despairing.

What Will You Choose?

What choice will you make about your day, **today**?

What choice will you make about your **future**?

Want To Know What's the Strongest, Most Powerful Choice We Can Make?

Choose **Love**, Always.

With Love at our side...

Everything else will take care of itself.

Thank you for your important question, and,

Happy Belated Birthday to you and to your friend.

WHAT'S NEXT?

Resources... To Keep Learning and Growing.

I hope you've enjoyed this Life Guide. It is "technically" complete, but I wanted to give you some **more resources on aging gracefully, self-love, and self-care** ... in case you'd like to continue the learning and the growing with me.

Here are some of my favorites — articles I've authored,[2] books I've written, and inspiring insights that I shared when I was interviewed by a reporter from the Weekend Today Show, to savor at your leisure.

Enjoy!

---

[2] All articles referenced in this section were published online.

AGING GRACEFULLY

Obsessing Over Wrinkles? Depressed About Aging?: 5 Questions To Help You Re-Focus on What Really Matters
— Published in Dr. Gelb's column, "All Grown Up" on Psychology Today.

https://www.psychologytoday.com/blog/all-grown/201502/obsessing-over-wrinkles-depressed-about-aging

Taking Care of an Elderly Parent -- and Not Loving It? How to Turn Resentment Into Patience and Joy
— Published on The Huffington Post.

http://www.huffingtonpost.com/dr-suzanne-gelb/caregiving_b_5260566.html

SELF LOVE

The Love Tune-Up: How to Amp Up the Love That's Naturally Inside You to Enjoy Happy, Healthy Relationships — A 14-Day Course That Can Change Your Life

https://amzn.to/2XQ7190

Welcome Home: Release Addictions and Return to Love

https://amzn.to/2vwXmIa

Ashamed of How You Look in a Swimsuit? Women: Please Read This
— Published on The Huffington Post.

https://www.huffpost.com/entry/post_n_5541682

Job Hunting and Your Body: How to Walk Into Your Next Interview With Confidence, Even When You Don't Love How You Look
— Published on The Huffington Post.

http://www.huffingtonpost.com/dr-suzanne-gelb/jobhunting-your-body-how-_b_5624321.html#es_share_ended

5 Ways to Stop Yourself from Eating When You're not Hungry
— Published on Psych Central.

http://psychcentral.com/blog/archives/2014/10/30/5-ways-to-stop-yourself-from-eating-when-youre-not-hungry/

Learning To Feed My Hungry Heart: My Journey From Bingeing To Wholeness
— Published Dr. Gelb's column, "All Grown Up" on Psychology Today.

https://www.psychologytoday.com/intl/blog/all-grown/201904/learning-feed-my-hungry-heart

SELF-CARE

You Are The Best Investment You'll Ever Make
— Published in Dr. Gelb's column, "All Grown Up" on Psychology Today.

https://www.psychologytoday.com/blog/all-grown/201511/you-are-the-best-investment-youll-ever-make

6 Self-Sabotaging Habits You Need To Drop Right Now
— Published on Mind Body Green.

https://www.mindbodygreen.com/0-14014/6-selfsabotaging-habits-you-need-to-drop-right-now.html

The Greatest Cheerleader One Can Have — Lives Within: How To Stay Strong When Not Everyone Is Cheering for our Success.
— Published in Dr. Gelb's column, "All Grown Up" on Psychology Today.

https://www.psychologytoday.com/us/blog/all-grown/201902/the-greatest-cheerleader-person-can-have-lives-within

If You Want to Make Tomorrow Less Stressful—Start Tonight
— Published in Dr. Gelb's column, "Be Well At Work, on The Muse.

https://www.themuse.com/advice/if-you-want-to-make-tomorrow-less-stressfulstart-tonight

Side note: The Muse is an award-winning online career resource, with over 4 million quality, professional members. I'm honored to have received the praise below, from Adrian Granzella Larssen, Editor-in-Chief, in response to an article I wrote for The Muse:

"Wow! This is fantastic stuff. You're clearly incredible at what you do, and I'm so thrilled to share your advice with our audience!"

Stressed Out at Work? How to Cope -- Without Turning to Food or Booze
— Published on The Huffington Post.

https://www.huffpost.com/entry/stressed-out-at-work-how_n_6711034

The Life Guide on How to Care for Yourself When You're a Caregiver for Somebody Else

http://drsuzannegelb.com/life-guide-care-for-yourself-caregiver/

Praise

I enjoyed your Caregivers Guide. It is appealing, well-organized and has great information.

—Dr. Mary Clark, PhD, psychologist

Dr. Gelb's "How to Care for Yourself Life Guide" is brilliant, helpful and so necessary.

Having myself been a caretaker four times, I can tell you that the last thing someone needs is one more overwhelming thing to do. You are already operating in a complete state of overwhelm and yet still need some support and an outlet.

Suzanne has created the perfect easy, but powerful. way to do something for yourself. The question prompts with fill-in-the-blanks, makes doing the work feel like a pleasurable outlet. Through her questions and suggestions it's as if she's walking along side you gently guiding you with her big, open, nonjudgemental heart.

If you are feeling the need for something supportive, but feel like you can't deal with even one more thing, this guide is a super gentle, but powerful way, might just be the answer.

—Tracy Baum-Finkel

Before, self-care wasn't a word I ever would have used — it felt selfish and indulgent... but after working through this guide, I see how easily I can make myself feel better — and how that helps me take better care of my loved ones.

I absolutely loved how this guide broke everything down, step by step. I never felt overwhelmed.

—Rebecca Rapple

How to Succeed Everywhere: 10 Tips for Balance at Work, Home, in Relationships
— Written by Shelby Marra, published online on NBC's Today.

Learn my top ten tips on how women [can apply to anyone] can become high achievers in whatever they do — at work, in romance and as a parent. For partners, the romance section in this article, can be especially insightful.

https://www.today.com/health/how-become-high-achieving-woman-work-your-relationship-parent-t33071

Side note: As my colleague, friend, and gifted writing teacher, Alex Franzen said: *"THIS IS AMAZING! Being interviewed by a reporter from NBC's Today Show? Uh, that's the big leagues!"*

Yes, that's what happened. Shelby Marra with NBC's Today Show in New York, requested an interview with me so that she could write this article featuring me, for TODAY.com's Successful Women series.

How Successful People Do More in 24 Hours Than the Rest of Us Do in a Week
— Published on Newsweek; also published on The Muse.

The content in this article is bound to inspire. Some of the topics I cover include: "Fully Commit," "Ban 'Friendly Interruptions' at All Costs," "Hang With Fellow Super-Achievers," and "Prevent Emotions From Building." It takes a self-loving person to take this type of positive action to further their success.

https://www.newsweek.com/career/how-successful-people-do-more-24-hours-rest-us-do-week

ABOUT THE AUTHOR

Dr. Suzanne Gelb, PhD, JD is a psychologist, life coach and author. She overcame her own **battle with negative stereotypes about aging** — and over the past 3-plus decades, she has helped people to learn to age gracefully, using tools like the ones in this book.

Dr. Gelb's inspiring insights on personal growth have been featured on more than 200 radio programs, 260 TV interviews, and online on Time, Newsweek, Forbes, The Huffington Post, NBC's Today, The Daily Love, Positively Positive, Mind Body Green, The Muse & many other places, as well.

She is a contributing writer to Psychology Today, where she has a regular column. Her first article published on her column was called, **"Obsessing Over Wrinkles? Depressed About Aging?: 5 Questions to Help You Re-Focus on What Really Matters."**

Dr. Gelb's expertise with aging extends to eldercare. Her article, **"Taking Care of an Elderly Parent -- and Not Loving It? How to Turn Resentment Into Patience and Joy,"** was published on the Huffington Post.

She believes that it is never too late to become the person you want to be. Strong. Confident. Calm. Creative. Free of all of the burdens that have held you back — no matter what happened in the past.

To learn more, visit www.DrSuzanneGelb.com

OTHER BOOKS BY THE AUTHOR

It Starts With You – How to Raise Happy, Successful Children by Becoming the Best Role-Model You Can Possibly Be. A Guidebook For Parents.

How to Get Your Kids to Cooperate and Help Them Become the Best Grown-Ups They Can Be. (A Life Guide.)

Helping Your Teen Make Healthy Choices About Dating and Sex. (A Life Guide.)

How to Get Ready to Be a Parent and Be the Best Mom or Dad You Can Possibly Be. (A Life Guide.)

How to Forgive the One Who Hurt You Most. (A Life Guide.)

How to Deal With People Who Drive You Absolutely Nuts. (A Life Guide.)

How to Navigate Being Single and Savor Your Dating Adventure. (A Life Guide.)

The Love Tune-Up: How to Amp Up the Love That's Naturally Inside You to Enjoy Happy, Healthy Relationships.

How to Rekindle That Spark and Create the Relationship and Sex Life That You Want. (A Life Guide.)

How to Find Work That You Love When You're Stuck in a Job That You Hate. (A Life Guide.)

How to Reach Your Ideal Weight Through Kindness, Not Craziness. (A Life Guide.)

Welcome Home: Release Addictions and Return to Love.

How to Care for Yourself When You're a Caregiver for Somebody Else. (A Life Guide.)

Real Men Don't Vacuum. And Other Misguided Myths That Cause Conflict in Relationships.

INDEX[3]

A

acceptance, 3
action, 15, 16, 44, 107
afraid, 14, 18, 22, 24, 71, 85, 86
aging body, 3, 14, 15, 21
anger, 10, 17, 20, 21, 22, 23, 67
angry, 2, 21, 24, 48

B

basic attitudes, 25
behavior change, 25
burden, 81, 82, 83, 84

C

catalyst, 4
catharsis, 20, 22, 27, 50
celebrate your life, 38
change, 1, 9, 21, 25, 27, 61, 88, 102
children, 53, 55, 70, 72, 76, 82, 85, 86, 87, 109
choice, 10, 83, 99, 100
choose, 5, 77, 95, 99, 100

communication, 86, 87
complete, 22, 23, 36, 51, 101
confident, 3, 108
correlation, 24, 27, 50
criticality, 31

D

different motivations, 30
disgusted, 2, 19

E

elderly, 82, 88, 102, 108
emotional "toolkit", 3
emotional healing process, 25
emotional well being, 8
empathize, 86
empowering, 9

F

fear(s), 1, 10, 13, 20, 22, 23, 30, 31, 34, 35, 38, 52, 67, 72, 73, 75, 78, 81, 83, 85, 87
frustrated, 2

---

[3] The page numbers in this index refer to the printed version of this book.

G

grace, 1, 11
gracefully, 64, 101, 102, 108
grandchild, 88
grandparent, 88
guided meditation, 30, 36

H

healing, 25, 50
heart, 4, 86, 87, 103, 106
heart-to-heart talk, 87
honor your body, 37

I

incomplete, 64
inner beauty, 15
inner battles with aging, 67
inner child, 50, 51, 72, 74
inner self, 13
inner wisdom, 21
insight(s), 25, 27, 30, 43, 72, 80, 101, 108
inspire, 61, 107
invisible, 2, 49, 51, 68

J

judgement, 17
judging, 94

L

look in the mirror, 2, 3, 12, 15, 19, 31, 32, 67

M

mortality, 14, 17, 73

N

negative attitudes, 3, 5, 7, 16, 17, 35
negative emotional energy, 10, 18
negative emotion(s), 3, 10, 17, 23, 27, 50, 58, 67
negative feelings, 11, 35, 50, 69
negative message, 84
negative thoughts, 36
new tools, 48, 67

O

older person, 55, 56
older people, 3, 7, 8, 61, 64
our needs, 86

P

personal growth work, 50
pessimistic outlook, 98
pound(ing) the pillow, 21, 22

R

release, 5, 10, 17, 18, 19, 20, 22, 36, 37
release anger, 22
resolve(d), 3, 10, 16, 35, 71, 78, 83
retire(ment), 90, 96, 97
rewrite the script, 27, 39

S

satisfaction, 66
savor your life and body, 6
script, 13, 25, 27, 39, 40, 45, 50, 51
self-acceptance, 40, 91
self-criticality, 17, 36
self-criticism, 3, 10, 31
self-directed anger, 17
self-esteem, 8, 84
self-judgement, 17, 91
self-loathing, 29, 30, 31, 35
self-love, 1, 3, 10, 11, 30, 31, 101
self-loving, 3, 107
self-pride, 30, 31
self-reflection, 10
self-worth, 8, 49, 84
somebody else, 3, 105, 109
somebody else's script, 13

T

the SHINE list, 61
three-step process, 18, 19, 27
3-step process, 23, 50, 52
true self, 42, 43, 44, 48, 49
trust, 21, 24, 87

U

ugly, 25, 30, 31, 43
unattractive, 25
understand(ing), 10, 30, 70, 72, 80, 85, 87

W

wrinkles, 3, 12, 20, 39, 102, 108
write and reflect, 12, 31

Y

young people, 90, 94
your body, 8, 9, 18, 20, 29, 36, 37, 40, 42, 44, 45, 67, 103
your true self, 42, 43, 44, 48, 49

www.ingramcontent.com/pod-product-compliance
Lightning Source LLC
Chambersburg PA
CBHW020141130526
44591CB00030B/172